Cousteau:

An Unauthorized Biography
by Kevin Comber

MAGIC BEAN
· IN - FACT ·

Contents

Introduction

Jacques-Yves Cousteau is a great sea explorer who believes that we need to care for sea life. He thinks we should not pollute our oceans and rivers by pouring rubbish into them.

Born: June 11, 1910 in St André-de-Cubzac, France

Father: Daniel

Mother: Elizabeth

Brother: Pierre

During his school life and as a young man, Cousteau developed a keen interest in diving. In 1930 he joined the French Navy. On one trip he saw a Chinese fisherman dive underwater and catch a fish with his bare hands. Cousteau thought this was amazing.

When he returned home, a friend gave him some goggles for underwater diving. Cousteau was fascinated by how many beautiful things he could see.

Some of Cousteau's important achievements are:
- inventing Self-Contained Underwater Breathing Apparatus (SCUBA) [see page 5];
- filming underwater;
- exploring the oceans;
- teaching people about conservation;
- being a peacemaker.

Inventing the SCUBA

In 1943 Cousteau and Emile Gagnan invented the SCUBA, which was the basis of modern diving equipment.

Using this equipment Cousteau could make deeper dives, stay under the water for a long time and move around more easily than with the old equipment.

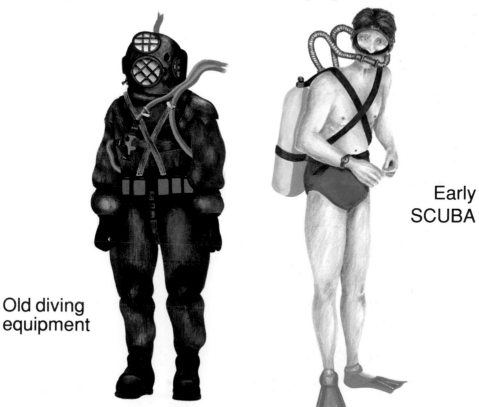

Early SCUBA

Old diving equipment

The first time Cousteau used the SCUBA, he did loops and somersaults underwater. He even stood upside down on one finger and burst out laughing.

Often Cousteau went diving with his family. Simone, his wife, was the world's first female SCUBA diver! Cousteau made special mini air tanks for his two sons.

Modern SCUBA

Filming underwater

In 1946 Cousteau started to make colour underwater films. This had not been done before. He needed to use lights because it was too dark to film in deep water. The colour and the beauty of the fish and plants amazed him.

Later Cousteau made a film called *The Silent World* which won an Academy Award. This film showed dolphins swimming alongside the ship, sharks feasting on a dead baby whale and divers exploring reefs and shipwrecks.

Cousteau also took photographs underwater. Once he lowered a camera 7 kms (4 miles) to the sea floor. There the ocean was so deep that you could almost fit Mount Everest below the surface! He discovered that starfish live at this depth.

Since 1966 Cousteau has made many television 'specials' about his adventures. He has said, "Each time we dive we learn something new."

He made films about elephant seals, marine iguanas, dolphins, grey whales, octopuses, squid, orcas (killer whales) and a film in the world's highest navigable lake, Lake Titicaca.

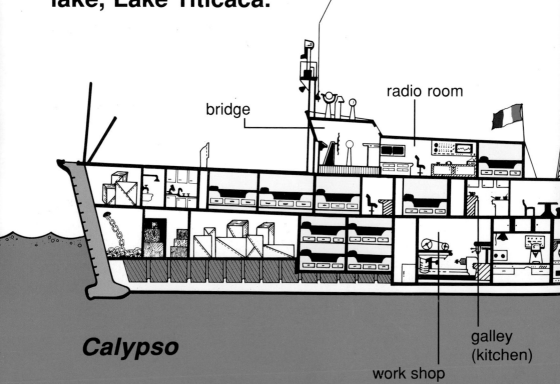

bridge

radio room

galley (kitchen)

work shop

Calypso

Exploring the oceans

Cousteau wanted to find out even more about life under the sea and whether or not people could live under water. In 1950 he was given a ship, called *Calypso*, to help him explore the oceans. He built a viewing section into the ship below the waterline, so he could see what was happening underwater. In 1959 Cousteau invented a mini submarine which carried two people. He called it the 'saucer'.

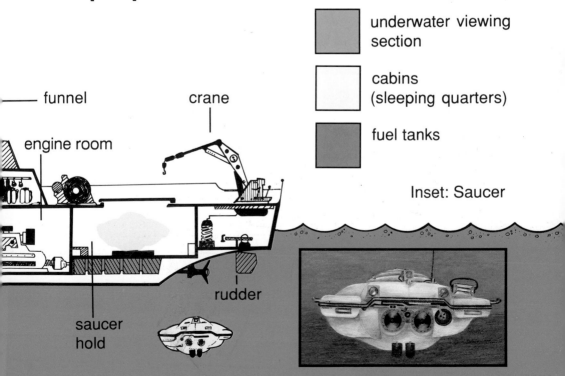

underwater viewing section

cabins (sleeping quarters)

fuel tanks

Inset: Saucer

funnel

crane

engine room

rudder

saucer hold

On Cousteau's first trip in the *Calypso* he explored the coral reefs of the Red Sea. There he found new fish and new kinds of plants. Cousteau filmed the Parrot fish charging the coral and biting off big chunks of it to eat.

sleeping quarters

The team had many adventures with whales. They discovered that humpback whales swam to one side of the divers almost as if they were taking care not to hurt them. A diver on Cousteau's ship once rode on the back of an orca!

Another way Cousteau and his team explored the ocean was by living in small metal houses under the sea. They could stay in these houses because air and electricity were piped down from a ship above.

During the days, they left the house and dived much deeper than they could have if they had started at the top. Cousteau thought that people in the future might live under the sea.

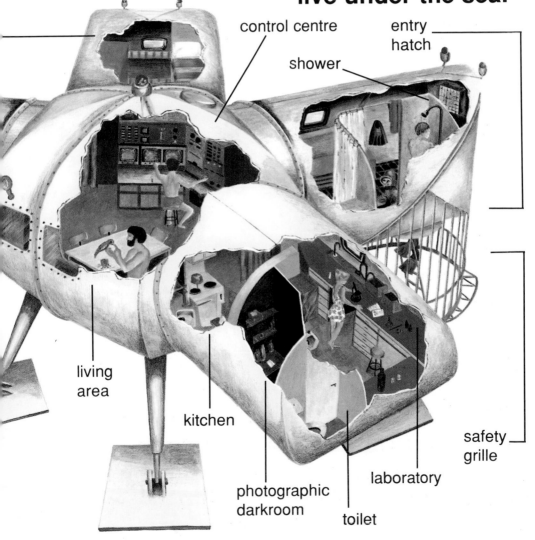

control centre

entry hatch

shower

living area

kitchen

photographic darkroom

toilet

laboratory

safety grille

Teaching people about conservation

Cousteau has always worked to help people understand conservation. He used the money he made from sales of the SCUBA, to find out more about the sea and to explain how people can care for the environment.

In 1960 the French Government wanted to dump nuclear rubbish into the sea. Cousteau fought this until they agreed not to pollute the sea. In 1961 he won the National Geographic Society Medal. The words ". . . he gave the key to the silent world" are written on the medal. He had shown life in the sea as no one had done before. Cousteau hoped this knowledge would help us save threatened animal and plant species. He has become more and more worried about rubbish (spilt oil, plastic, etc.) found in the sea. He also realized that too much fishing was going on and he warned that many kinds of fish would become extinct.

In 1982 Cousteau's team decided to explore the world's biggest river, the Amazon. This river was still fairly clean and they discovered river dolphins, frogs "as big as a thumb nail" and monkeys weighing only "as much as an egg"! They also saw spiders "big enough to catch birds"!

Sea otter rescued from an oil spill

In 1990 Cousteau took a group of six children to Antarctica. He wanted to show them the unspoilt beauty of that frozen world. He believes this area should be protected from mining. Cousteau is trying to get countries to agree to keep Antarctica as a world park that will not be changed or destroyed by people.

Emperor penguin rookery in Antarctica

Being a peacemaker

A few years ago, Cousteau thought about ways to save the world from war. He suggested that children about seven years old should live in another country for a year, a country unfriendly to theirs. Then those countries might not drop bombs on each other because their own children would be living there.

Conclusion

When he was seventy-five, on June 11, 1985, Cousteau had a special birthday in Washington D.C., U.S.A. All his family and friends were there and the crew from the *Calypso*. He did not want too much of a fuss. "Monkeys and mosquitoes don't have birthdays," he said.

Cousteau is still working as hard as ever. He is still interested in the sea and in saving our world from pollution. He is still travelling and showing us wonders of nature.